Though I Walk through the Valley

12 DAYS IN PSALM 23

LAUREN FLAKE

FOR CARLY, LAUREN, MEGHAN, JENNIFER, AND TERRI,
WHOSE FRIENDSHIP HELPED ME SURVIVE A PANDEMIC

loveofdixie

CONTENTS

INTRODUCTION

THE MOST WELL-KNOWN OF ALL THE PSALMS, PSALM 23 IS ATTRIBUTED TO KING DAVID AND WAS USED IN ANCIENT HEBREW WORSHIP.

A HUMBLE SHEPHERD IN HIS YOUTH, BEFORE HE MADE HISTORY BY SLAYING GOLIATH AND IMPREGNATING BATHSHEBA, DAVID UNDERSTOOD THE RUGGED AND DIRTY WORK INVOLVED IN PROTECTING AND PROVIDING FOR A FLOCK OF SHEEP IN THE WILDERNESS.

(THINK TEXAS COWBOY DEALING WITH CACTUS, COYOTES, WATER MOCCASINS, AND RATTLESNAKES WHEN THEY STILL WENT ON ACTUAL CATTLE DRIVES, MINUS THE SAFETY OF THE HORSE AND CHUCKWAGON.)

HE WAS RESPONSIBLE FOR KEEPING TABS ON THE LOCATION AND HEALTH OF EVERY ANIMAL IN HIS CARE. LIKEWISE, GOD KEEPS TABS ON US, GUIDING AND CORRECTING US AT EVERY TURN IF WE WILL ONLY SUBMIT TO HIS AUTHORITY AND TRUST IN HIS GOODNESS AND LOVING MERCY. EASIER SAID THAN DONE, RIGHT?

OUR SPIRIT CRAVES HIS GOODNESS AND WISDOM, BUT OUR FLESH WANTS TO REBEL AND ASSERT OUR INDEPENDENCE. WE ARE LIKE STUBBORN TODDLERS SAYING, "ME DO IT," WHEN WE REALLY NEED MOMMA'S HELP TO GET INTO THAT CHAIR. WE ARE LIKE STUBBORN SHEEP WITHOUT THE NECESSARY PROTECTION AND GUIDANCE OF A SHEPHERD:

"WE ALL, LIKE SHEEP, HAVE GONE ASTRAY, EACH OF US HAS TURNED TO OUR OWN WAY; AND THE LORD HAS LAID ON HIM THE INIQUITY OF US ALL." (ISAIAH 53:6 NIV)

IN MATTHEW, WE READ, "WHEN HE [JESUS] SAW THE CROWDS, HE HAD COMPASSION ON THEM, BECAUSE THEY WERE HARASSED AND HELPLESS, LIKE SHEEP WITHOUT A SHEPHERD." (MATTHEW 9:36 NIV)

JESUS KNEW THAT SUBMISSION TO HIM MEANS FREEDOM AND NEW LIFE FOR US. GOD IS THE GOOD AND PERFECT SHEPHERD IN THE WILDERNESS OF CONFUSION, PAIN, AND GRIEF WE SO OFTEN FACE THIS SIDE OF HEAVEN. AS WE WALK THROUGH PSALM 23 TOGETHER, MY PRAYER IS THAT WE WILL LEARN TO TRUST HIM ALONE AS OUR GOOD SHEPHERD AND STOP RELYING ON OURSELVES.

(ACCORDING TO W. PHILLIP KELLER, PSALM 23 REPRESENTS A FULL YEAR OF A SHEPHERD STEWARDING HIS SHEEP. I'VE ATTEMPTED TO DIVIDE THE VERSES INTO SEASONS TO HELP YOU GET A BIGGER OVERVIEW OF THE SCRIPTURE.)

DAY 1

TRUTH

The Lord is my shepherd.
Psalm 23:1 NIV

I WROTE THE FIRST DRAFT OF MY MOTHER'S OBITUARY ON A BRIGHT, YELLOW LEGAL PAD. I SAT ON AN EMPTY BED IN A NURSING HOME ACROSS FROM MY MOM'S UNCONSCIOUS BODY, WATCHING HER TAKE LABORED BREATHS IN HER FINAL DAYS. THE FAITH THAT CARRIED ME THROUGH HER DECADE OF DECLINE INTO EARLY ONSET ALZHEIMER'S DISEASE WAS THE ONLY THING THAT SUSTAINED ME THROUGH HER PASSING.

EMBEDDED IN THE CENTER OF HER OBITUARY IS WHAT I CONSIDER TO BE MY LIFE VERSE, THE WORDS SHE HAD WRITTEN ON THE DEDICATION PAGE OF THE NIV STUDY BIBLE SHE GAVE ME FOR CHRISTMAS WHEN I WAS IN MIDDLE SCHOOL:

"THEN YOU WILL KNOW THE TRUTH, AND THE TRUTH WILL SET YOU FREE." (JOHN 8:32 NIV)

I HAD NO IDEA THE POWER OF THESE WORDS AS A NAÏVE, CHURCH-GOING PRETEEN. THE TRUTH SURELY SET MY MOTHER FREE AS HER LIFE ON EARTH ENDED—FREE FROM PAIN AND SUFFERING, FROM DEPRESSION AND ANXIETY, AND FROM A DEVASTATING DISEASE—BUT IT ALSO SET ME FREE TO MATURE SPIRITUALLY WITHOUT HER.

KNOWING TRUTH BEGINS WITH RECOGNIZING OUR DEPRAVITY AND INCOMPETENCE IN CONTRAST WITH GOD'S PERFECT SOVEREIGNTY AND PROVISION. WHEN I DEPENDED UPON MY MOTHER AS MY MENTOR AND TEACHER, I DID NOT SEE MY NEED TO DEPEND FULLY ON JESUS FOR SUSTENANCE. I DID NOT UNDERSTAND THE NECESSITY OF MEDITATING ON HIS PROMISES AND CHOOSING TO FOLLOW HIM INSTEAD OF THE WORLD OVER AND OVER AGAIN EACH DAY.

"I AM THE GOOD SHEPHERD. THE GOOD SHEPHERD LAYS DOWN HIS LIFE FOR THE SHEEP." (JOHN 10:11 NIV)

DO YOU BELIEVE THAT GOD IS YOUR GOOD AND PERFECT SHEPHERD? WHY OR WHY NOT? WHO OR WHAT ARE YOU DEPENDING ON INSTEAD?

DAY 2

CONTENTMENT

I lack nothing.
Psalm 23:1

MY GREAT-GRANDMOTHER'S ANTIQUE PLATE DISPLAYED IN MY DINING ROOM READS, IN BEAUTIFUL, GILDED LETTERS SURROUNDED BY ROSES, "GIVE US THIS DAY OUR DAILY BREAD."

AS A KID, I KNEW THIS WAS A SAYING FROM THE LORD'S PRAYER. NOW, I UNDERSTAND THAT IT IS A PROFESSION OF FAITH IN AND GRATITUDE FOR GOD'S PROVISION OF MANNA FROM HEAVEN FOR THE ISRAELITES WANDERING IN THE DESERT. HE GAVE THEM ONLY WHAT THEY NEEDED FOR EACH DAY, DESPITE THEIR WHINING AND COMPLAINING, AND HE WILL DO THE SAME FOR US.

CONTENTMENT IS OUR ACCEPTANCE OF OUR CURRENT CIRCUMSTANCES. IT IS THE END OF STRIVING, COMPARISON, AND JEALOUSY AND THE BEGINNING OF PEACE AND REST. CONTENTMENT IS BELIEVING THAT GOD WILL GIVE US WHAT WE NEED AND NOT WANTING MORE THAN HE PROVIDES.

IT IS NOT WORRYING ABOUT TOMORROW. IT IS CRAVING HIM ALONE INSTEAD OF A NEW, MORE RELIABLE CAR, OR MORE OBEDIENT KIDS, OR A BETTER-PAYING JOB, OR A BIGGER, CLEANER HOUSE. IT IS LETTING GOD BE ENOUGH FOR TODAY.

"I HAVE LEARNED TO BE CONTENT WHATEVER THE CIRCUMSTANCES." (PHILIPPIANS 4:1 NIV)

ARE YOU CONTENT IN HIS GOODNESS, OR ARE YOU STRIVING FOR MORE THAN HE PROVIDES YOU WITH TODAY?

SPRING

DAY 3

REST

He makes me lie down in green pastures.
Psalm 23:2

I BELIEVE THIS SECOND VERSE REPRESENTS THE SHEPHERD AND FLOCK'S SEASON OF SPRINGTIME AND RENEWAL AT HOME.

DO YOU STRUGGLE TO BE STILL AND REST WHEN GOD GIVES YOU THE OPPORTUNITY? I REMEMBER WHEN I STARTED DOING YOGA AT THE END OF COLLEGE, I COULD NOT IMAGINE WHY I WOULD WASTE MY TIME AT THE END OF EACH SESSION LAYING ON THE FLOOR, NOT MOVING.

NOW, I LOVE SAVASANA, OR CORPSE POSE—THOSE PRECIOUS FIVE MINUTES AT THE END OF MY YOGA PRACTICE. I USE THAT TIME TO CLEAR MY MIND, RELAX MY BODY, AND TALK TO GOD, FULLY PRESENT IN THE MOMENT, THANKING HIM FOR STICKING WITH ME IN ALL OF MY REBELLION, ARROGANCE, AND IMPATIENCE.

GOD KNOWS THAT WE NEED REST BUILT INTO OUR WEEKLY SCHEDULES. THAT'S WHY HE RESTED ON THE SEVENTH DAY. THAT'S WHY HE REQUIRES SABBATH. HE GIVES US FREEDOM IN SUBMITTING TO HIM AND ALLOWING OURSELVES TO REST IN HIS LEADERSHIP.

JESUS TOLD HIS DISCIPLES:

"COME TO ME, ALL YOU WHO ARE WEARY AND BURDENED, AND I WILL GIVE YOU REST. TAKE MY YOKE UPON YOU AND LEARN FROM ME, FOR I AM GENTLE AND HUMBLE IN HEART, AND YOU WILL FIND REST FOR YOUR SOULS. FOR MY YOKE IS EASY AND MY BURDEN IS LIGHT." (MATTHEW 11:28-30 NIV)

THEY WOULD HAVE EASILY UNDERSTOOD THE PICTURE THE SON OF GOD PAINTED WITH HIS WORDS. FARMERS WORKED THEIR FIELDS WITH A PAIR OF OXEN—ONE MATURE OX TO LEAD THE EFFORT AND ONE YOUNG OX TO LEARN FROM THE OTHER.

THIS PASSAGE ALWAYS MAKES ME THINK OF TAVIA IN FIDDLER ON THE ROOF SINGING AND WORKING DILIGENTLY BUT JOYFULLY TO PROVIDE FOR HIS FAMILY.

DEPENDING UPON JESUS INSTEAD OF OURSELVES MAKES OUR BURDEN LIGHT. THE PAIN AND STRUGGLE DOESN'T NECESSARILY GO AWAY, BUT IT BECOMES MANAGEABLE INSTEAD OF DEBILITATING WHEN WE LET HIM CARRY THE WEIGHT AND REST IN HIS LEADERSHIP.

HOW ARE YOU ACCEPTING HIS INVITATION TO REST?

DAY 4

PROVIDENCE

He leads me beside quiet waters.
Psalm 23:2

ONE OF MY FAVORITE BLUE OCTOBER SONGS IS CALLED "A QUIET MIND." I ABSOLUTELY CLUNG TO ITS LYRICS THROUGHOUT MY MENTAL HEALTH STRUGGLES IN COLLEGE.

MY STRUGGLE WITH ANXIETY AND SHAME BEGAN WAY BACK IN PRESCHOOL. WORRY ABOUT TOMORROW IS JUST THE TIP OF THE ICEBERG FOR ME. IN HIGH SCHOOL, I USED TO LAY AWAKE WORRYING ABOUT WHAT WAS UNDER THE TOP COAT OF PAINT ON MY 1950S BEDROOM WINDOW FRAME. I USED TO WORRY THAT I COULD ONLY DEPEND ON ME TO KEEP ME SAFE.

IT HAS TAKEN ME THREE DECADES TO LEARN TO TRUST GOD TO CARE FOR ME. HE MEETS MY NEEDS FAR MORE ADEQUATELY THAN I COULD EVER KNOW HOW TO WATCH OUT FOR MYSELF AND ANTICIPATE TRAGEDIES BEFORE THEY HAPPEN.

GOD IS THE GOOD SHEPHERD AND THE PERFECT FATHER. HE CARES DEEPLY FOR EACH OF HIS SHEEP, OR PRECIOUS, VULNERABLE CHILDREN. IN PERFECT LOVE, HE IS ALWAYS FOR US AND NEVER AGAINST US. HE PROTECTS US AND ANTICIPATES OUR NEEDS. HE CARES FOR US, PERSONALLY AND INTIMATELY, ON BOTH A CORPORATE AND INDIVIDUAL LEVEL. HIS LOVE FOR HIS FLOCK AND FOR EACH AND EVERY ONE OF HIS SHEEP KNOWS NO BOUNDS.

JOB DESCRIBED GOD'S FAITHFULNESS TO HIM DURING RIDICULOUS AMOUNTS OF GRIEF AND TEMPTATION TO SIN: "YOU GAVE ME LIFE AND SHOWED ME KINDNESS, AND IN YOUR PROVIDENCE WATCHED OVER MY SPIRIT." (JOB 10:12 NIV)

EVEN WHEN IT SEEMED THAT JOB WAS LOSING EVERYTHING— HIS LIVESTOCK, HIS FRIENDS, HIS CHILDREN, AND HIS HEALTH —HE CONTINUED TO TRUST AND PRAISE GOD FOR HIS PROVIDENCE. HE KNEW THAT GOD ALWAYS PROVIDES, EVEN WHEN IT DOES NOT LOOK THE WAY WE EXPECT IN THE END.

HE DID NOT WORRY ABOUT TOMORROW, AND NEITHER SHOULD
WE.

ARE YOU WORRIED ABOUT THE CIRCUMSTANCES OF YOUR FINITE
FUTURE? HOW CAN YOU TRUST MORE FULLY IN HIS INFINITE
CARE AND PROVIDENCE FOR ETERNITY INSTEAD?

SUMMER

DAY 5

TRANSFORMATION

He refreshes my soul.
Psalm 23:3

AS A KID, I LOVED TRAVELING WITH MY FAMILY EACH WINTER TO WEST TEXAS FOR A HUGE CHURCH RETREAT CALLED STREAM IN THE DESERT. THE OLDER I BECAME, THE MORE I LOVED (AND NEEDED) THAT BEAUTIFUL MENTAL IMAGE OF REFRESHMENT BY A FLOWING STREAM IN A DRY LAND.

CAN YOU IMAGINE THE BEAUTY OF FINDING A FRESH STREAM FOR A PARCHED SHEPHERD TENDING HIS THIRSTY FLOCK IN THE HEAT OF SUMMER?

WE KNOW THAT JESUS' LIVING WATER NEVER RUNS OUT; THIS IS WHAT HE PROMISED THE SAMARITAN WOMAN AT THE WELL. HE DOES NOT SIMPLY QUENCH OUR PHYSICAL THIRST BUT ALSO OUR SPIRITUAL THIRST, IF WE SIMPLY BELIEVE IN HIM, TRUST HIM, AND COME TO HIM FOR LIVING WATER.

PAUL WROTE TO THE CHURCH IN ROME, WHO STRUGGLED WITH BUILDING THEIR NEW MINISTRY IN A CULTURE HEAVILY SATURATED WITH ANCIENT PAGANISM:

"DO NOT CONFORM TO THE PATTERN OF THIS WORLD, BUT BE TRANSFORMED BY THE RENEWING OF YOUR MIND. THEN YOU WILL BE ABLE TO TEST AND APPROVE WHAT GOD'S WILL IS— HIS GOOD, PLEASING AND PERFECT WILL." (ROMANS 12:2 NIV)

WE CAN'T CHANGE THE WORLD WHEN WE LOOK JUST LIKE IT. WE MUST BE CONTINUALLY RENEWED AND TRANSFORMED TO STAND OUT.

HOW ARE YOU INVITING GOD TO TRANSFORM YOUR HEART AND MIND? HOW CAN YOU MAKE THIS A DAILY HABIT?

DAY 6

PURPOSE

He guides me along the right paths for his name's sake.
Psalm 23:3

I HAVE OFTEN BEEN GUILTY OF THINKING THAT WHEN THIS CURRENT DIFFICULT SEASON OF GRIEF, MOTHERHOOD, AND CAREGIVING IS OVER, I WILL BE ABLE TO DO MY "REAL WORK" FOR GOD'S KINGDOM. I CONVINCE MYSELF THAT I WILL FIND AND PURSUE MY TRUE CALLING WHEN I HAVE MORE TIME AND EMOTIONAL ENERGY.

THE TRUTH IS THAT WE WASTE SO MUCH TIME SEARCHING FOR OUR CALLING. FRIENDS, THIS IS YOUR CALLING: "GO AND MAKE DISCIPLES." (MATTHEW 28:19 NIV) THAT'S IT, PLAIN AND SIMPLE.

NOW, WHAT ARE YOUR PASSIONS AND TALENTS? WELL, THAT'S A DIFFERENT CONVERSATION. YOUR PURPOSE IS MINISTRY— LOVING GOD AND HIS PEOPLE WELL. SURE, YOU CAN USE THOSE PASSIONS AND TALENTS TO FULFILL THAT PURPOSE AS YOU FIGURE THEM OUT, BUT IT'S THE "WHY," NOT THE "HOW," THAT'S THE KEY:

"AND WE KNOW THAT IN ALL THINGS GOD WORKS FOR THE GOOD OF THOSE WHO LOVE HIM, WHO HAVE BEEN CALLED ACCORDING TO HIS PURPOSE." (ROMANS 8:28 NIV)

WHEN WE'RE FOCUSED ON THAT HIGHER PURPOSE AND OPEN AND OBEDIENT TO HIS CALL, HE WILL PUT US IN SITUATIONS AND GIVE US OPPORTUNITIES WHERE WE CAN USE OUR GIFTS TO SERVE HIM. IN FACT, HE'S PROBABLY ALREADY PLACED US THERE. WE NEED ONLY TO TRUST HIM AND BE WILLING TO SAY "YES" WHEREVER HE LEADS US.

AS A GARDENER, I LOVE TO FOLLOW THE MANTRA, "BLOOM WHERE GOD PLANTS YOU." STOP WORRYING SO MUCH ABOUT WHERE YOU ARE SUPPOSED TO BE AND PAY MORE ATTENTION TO WHAT YOU ARE SUPPOSED TO BE DOING WHERE YOU ALREADY ARE.

IT'S LIKE MOTHER TERESA SAID, "IF YOU WANT TO CHANGE THE WORLD, GO HOME AND LOVE YOUR FAMILY." OR, AS THEODORE ROOSEVELT SAID, "DO WHAT YOU CAN, WITH WHAT YOU HAVE, WHERE YOU ARE."

ARE YOU BLOOMING, OR SERVING GOD AND HIS PEOPLE, WHERE YOU'RE PLANTED? IF YES, HOW? IF NOT, HOW CAN YOU START RIGHT NOW?

AUTUMN

DAY 7

PEACE

Even though I walk through the darkest valley, I will fear no evil, for you are with me.

Psalm 23:4

HERE, DAVID IS PREPARING HIS FLOCK FOR THE HARDSHIP OF WINTER BY MOVING THEM.

I AM AN ENNEAGRAM TYPE 6. MY DEEPEST FEAR IS LACK OF SUPPORT. I AM PRONE TO ANXIETY AND HAVE A DEEP NEED FOR SECURITY. I AM CONSTANTLY CHECKING MY SURROUNDINGS AND LOOKING FOR POTENTIAL PROBLEMS. I AM STILL LEARNING TO CHOOSE FAITH OVER FEAR EACH DAY.

THE IMPRISONED APOSTLE PAUL WROTE TO THE CHURCH AT PHILIPPI:

"DO NOT BE ANXIOUS ABOUT ANYTHING, BUT IN EVERY SITUATION, BY PRAYER AND PETITION, WITH THANKSGIVING, PRESENT YOUR REQUESTS TO GOD. AND THE PEACE OF GOD, WHICH TRANSCENDS ALL UNDERSTANDING, WILL GUARD YOUR HEARTS AND YOUR MINDS IN CHRIST JESUS." (PHILIPPIANS 4:6-7 NIV)

I ABSOLUTELY LOVE THAT IMAGE OF GOD GUARDING MY HEART AND MIND FROM DARKNESS AND EVIL. WHEN I REMEMBER TO MEDITATE ON THIS PROMISE, INSTEAD OF ALLOWING MYSELF TO PANIC, I FIND HIS PERFECT PEACE, AND MY SOUL FINDS REST.

ONLY THEN DO I "FEAR NO EVIL" AND FEEL THE PROTECTIVE PRESENCE OF HIS HOLY SPIRIT DEEP WITHIN ME.

HOW ARE YOU LIVING IN FEAR, OR, ALTERNATELY, HOW ARE YOU WALKING BY FAITH EACH DAY?

DAY 8

OBEDIENCE

Your rod and your staff,
they comfort me.
Psalm 23:4 NIV

MY GRANDMOTHER WROTE IN MY MOTHER'S BABY BOOK THAT THE FIRST SONG MY MOM EVER MEMORIZED AS A CHILD WAS THE OLD CHURCH HYMN, 'TRUST AND OBEY':

"WHEN WE WALK WITH THE LORD
IN THE LIGHT OF HIS WORD,
WHAT A GLORY HE SHEDS ON OUR WAY;
WHILE WE DO HIS GOOD WILL,
HE ABIDES WITH US STILL,
AND WITH ALL WHO WILL TRUST AND OBEY.

TRUST AND OBEY,
FOR THERE'S NO OTHER WAY
TO BE HAPPY IN JESUS,
BUT TO TRUST AND OBEY. ..."

AS A CHILD, I SAW OBEDIENCE AS A CHORE, BUT OBEDIENCE TO A PERFECT FATHER WHO KNOWS WHAT IS BEST FOR ME IS A NATURAL ACCEPTANCE OF HIS LOVE. SUBMISSION THROUGH OBEDIENCE ACTUALLY BRINGS FREEDOM, NOT BURDEN OR CAPTIVITY.

THE OLD TESTAMENT IS HEAVY ON OBEDIENCE: "OBSERVE THE COMMANDS OF THE LORD YOUR GOD, WALKING IN OBEDIENCE TO HIM AND REVERING HIM." (DEUTERONOMY 8:6 NIV)

THE NEW TESTAMENT SHOWS US THAT WE HAVE A NEW COMMANDMENT TO FOLLOW INSTEAD: "LOVE ONE ANOTHER." (JOHN 13:34 NIV)

YET, WE OFTEN OVERLOOK THE FACT THAT THE TEN COMMANDMENTS ARE PART OF FOLLOWING THAT NEW LAW. EVERY ONE OF THOSE GUIDELINES FITS THE CRITERIA OF "LOVE GOD. LOVE PEOPLE." FOLLOWING THEM SIMPLY HELPS US FULFILL THAT HIGHER PURPOSE OF SHARING HIS LOVE.

ARE YOU FOLLOWING HIS COMMANDMENTS TO LOVE GOD AND LOVE HIS PEOPLE? WHO CAN YOU LOVE WELL TODAY?

HOLIDAYS

DAY 9

GRATITUDE

You prepare a table before me in the presence of my enemies.
Psalm 23:5

I FIND IT HUMOROUS THAT SHEPHERDS COMMONLY FED THEIR SHEEP ON RAISED TABLES BECAUSE WE FEED OUR BLACK LAB AND FED OUR PREVIOUS LABS ON A RAISED FEEDER MY HUSBAND BUILT. IT IS SIMPLY BETTER FOR THEIR DIGESTION AND EASIER ON THEIR JOINTS FOR THEM NOT TO HAVE TO BEND DOWN SO FAR TO EAT.

MY BEST FRIEND SAYS I HAVE "GOLD-PLATED DOGS." THEY ARE WELL CARED FOR, THAT'S FOR SURE. ARE THEY SPOILED? MAYBE.

MY AFFECTIONATE, LOYAL DOGS WERE MY FIRST BABIES. MY HUSBAND AND I ADOPTED THEM AS PUPPIES, LONG BEFORE WE HAD HUMAN CHILDREN. I LOVED THEM AND DELIGHTED IN PROVIDING FOR THEIR NEEDS.

THINK HOW MUCH MORE GOD MUST DELIGHT IN CARING FOR US, THE BEST OF HIS CREATION. OUR GRATITUDE IS SIMPLY A SMALL OFFERING IN RETURN WHEN HE FREELY LAVISHES HIS LOVE ON US AND PROVIDES FOR OUR NEEDS.

JUST AS MY DOGS PROVIDE SLOBBERY KISSES, LAY AT MY FEET, AND SHOW UP WITH WAGGING TAILS WHEN I RETURN HOME, MAY WE DELIGHT IN AND SHOW APPRECIATION FOR THE GOODNESS OF OUR FATHER:

"LET THE MESSAGE OF CHRIST DWELL AMONG YOU RICHLY AS YOU TEACH AND ADMONISH ONE ANOTHER WITH ALL WISDOM THROUGH PSALMS, HYMNS, AND SONGS FROM THE SPIRIT, SINGING TO GOD WITH GRATITUDE IN YOUR HEARTS." (COLOSSIANS 3:16 NIV)

HOW ARE YOU GIVING THANKS AND DELIGHTING IN HIS GOODNESS EACH DAY?

DAY 10

PROTECTION

You anoint my head with oil.
Psalm 23:5

SHEPHERDS POURED OIL ON THE HEADS OF THEIR SHEEP IN ORDER TO DOCTOR THEIR WOUNDS AND PROTECT THEM FROM FLIES, GNATS, AND MOSQUITOES, PARTICULARLY IN THE SUMMER BUT PROBABLY ALSO IN THE LATE SPRING AND EARLY FALL. IT REMINDS ME OF HOW MY YOUNGEST DAUGHTER ASKS ME TO RUB HER BEDTIME BLEND OF ESSENTIAL OILS ON HER FOREHEAD, CHEST, AND FEET EACH NIGHT.

I QUITE LITERALLY ANOINT HER WITH OIL. I AM NOT PROTECTING HER FROM BUGS, ALTHOUGH WE DO HAVE AN OILS BLEND WE USE OUTSIDE TO DETER MOSQUITOES, BUT I AM HELPING HER RELAX AND FALL ASLEEP AS SHE COUNTS HER SHEEP (PUN INTENDED). I DO IT BECAUSE I LOVE HER AND WANT THE BEST FOR HER. I WANT HER TO SLEEP PEACEFULLY. I WANT TO PROTECT HER FROM HARM, IN THIS CASE, THE POTENTIAL FOR INSOMNIA AND BAD DREAMS.

WHEN I STARTED DRIVING AN OLD, BLUE AND SILVER '89 CHEVY SUBURBAN BY MYSELF AT AGE 16, MY MOM GAVE ME A PEWTER KEYCHAIN INSCRIBED WITH THIS VERSE: "FOR HE WILL COMMAND HIS ANGELS CONCERNING YOU TO GUARD YOU IN ALL YOUR WAYS." (PSALM 91:11 NIV)

LET'S JUST SAY I WAS NOT THE BEST DRIVER AS A TEENAGER. I WAS SOMEHOW BOTH IMPULSIVE AND HESITANT AT THE SAME TIME, WHICH IS A REALLY SCARY COMBINATION IN AUSTIN TRAFFIC. I WILL NEVER FORGET SOME OF THE TIMES I KNEW I SHOULD HAVE BEEN IN A WRECK BUT HIS PROTECTION SPARED ME.

HOW HAS GOD PROTECTED YOU FROM HARM IN THE PAST? DOES THIS HELP YOU TRUST HIM TO WATCH OVER YOU IN THE FUTURE?

WINTER

DAY 11

JOY

My cup overflows.
Psalm 23:5

ONLY A FULL CUP CAN OVERFLOW. NO, I AM NOT TALKING ABOUT SELF CARE, ALTHOUGH THAT HAS ITS PLACE WHEN IT IS CHRIST-CENTERED. I AM TALKING INSTEAD ABOUT THE INTERNAL, DEEP ABIDING JOY FOUND ONLY IN JESUS, DESPITE EXTERNAL CIRCUMSTANCES THAT MIGHT BE TERRIBLE. I AM TALKING ABOUT TRUSTING GOD IN THE MIDDLE OF OUR PAIN TO THE POINT OF BEING GRATEFUL FOR OUR STRUGGLE.

WHILE IMPRISONED, PAUL INSTRUCTED THE BELIEVERS AT PHILIPPI TO LIVE THEIR FAITH OUT LOUD FOR ALL TO SEE:

"REJOICE IN THE LORD ALWAYS. I WILL SAY IT AGAIN: REJOICE! LET YOUR GENTLENESS BE EVIDENT TO ALL. THE LORD IS NEAR." (PHILIPPIANS 4:4-5 NIV)

I WAS RAISED IN THE CHURCH BUT I DID NOT UNDERSTAND THIS CONCEPT UNTIL EXPERIENCING SEVERAL ROUNDS OF DEMENTIA CAREGIVING AND GRIEF AND LOSS IN ADULTHOOD.

WE ARE CALLED TO LIVE LIKE JESUS IS COMING BACK ALWAYS, DESPITE THE WORST OF EARTHLY CIRCUMSTANCES. GOD HEARS OUR CRIES, COUNTS OUR TEARS, AND FEELS OUR PAIN, YET HE MAKES OUR JOY COMPLETE. HE WANTS OTHERS WHO LACK FAITH TO SEE OUR JOY AND WANT TO GRASP HOLD OF IT FOR THEMSELVES.

LOVE, HOPE, AND JOY ARE CONTAGIOUS. THEY ARE HIS GOODNESS ON DISPLAY FOR ALL TO SEE.

DAVID WAS ABLE TO WORSHIP GOD IN THE WILDERNESS OF HIS DIFFICULT AND SOLITARY WORK BECAUSE HE HAD FIRST WORSHIPED GOD IN THE SANCTUARY AS A CHILD. HE ALREADY HAD AN INTIMATE, PERSONAL RELATIONSHIP WITH THE LORD THAT HE COULD CALL UPON IN TIMES OF BOTH HAPPINESS AND OF FEAR AND STRUGGLE.

HOW HAVE YOU FOUND HIS DEEP AND CONTAGIOUS JOY IN YOUR LIFE? IF YOU HAVE NOT, WHAT IS HOLDING YOU BACK?

NEW YEAR

DAY 12

CONFIDENCE

Surely your goodness and love will follow me all the days of my life, and I will dwell in the house of the Lord Forever.

Psalm 23:6

I AM REMINDED IN TIMES OF IMMENSE TROUBLE THAT THIS WORLD IS NOT MY HOME. UNFORTUNATELY, WHEN THINGS ARE GOING WELL, I HAVE A TENDENCY TO FORGET THIS TRUTH. I GET CAUGHT UP IN THINGS LIKE CONSUMERISM, COMPETITION, AND APPEARANCE. I BEGIN TO FOCUS ON MYSELF AND THE HERE AND NOW—ON HOW MY HOUSE LOOKS, OR HOW SUCCESSFULLY MY CAREER IS GROWING, OR HOW WELL MY MARRIAGE IS GOING, OR HOW MUCH MY KIDS ARE LEARNING AT SCHOOL.

WE STORE UP TEMPORARY TREASURES THAT WILL ULTIMATELY ROT AND DISINTEGRATE. WE ARE NOT SO DIFFERENT FROM THE EGYPTIAN PHARAOHS, HOARDING OUR WEALTH IN OUR PYRAMIDS SO THAT WE CAN USE IT IN THE AFTERLIFE.

YET, HEAVEN, NOT EARTH, IS WHERE WE LONG TO SPEND ETERNITY. GOD IS PREPARING A PLACE FOR US. NO AMOUNT OF OUR OWN SAVING, THRIFTING, PERFECTING, AND HOARDING CAN GET US THERE.

OUR ETERNAL REWARD IS NOT HERE. IT'S IN HEAVEN WITH OUR PERFECT FATHER:

"SO DO NOT THROW AWAY YOUR CONFIDENCE; IT WILL BE RICHLY REWARDED." (HEBREWS 10:35 NIV)

THE GOOD SHEPHERD AWAITS HIS FLOCK.

HOW WILL YOU KEEP YOUR FOCUS ON THINGS ABOVE AS YOU LIVE HERE ON EARTH EACH DAY?

ALSO AVAILABLE FROM
Lauren Flake

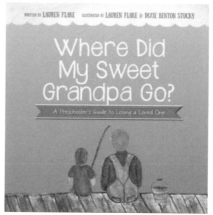

LaurenFlake.com/books